Hey Nail Friend,

You are Amazing!

THIS NAIL BOOK WAS CREATED FOR YOU, CLAIM IT!!!

MY NAME IS

I am on a mission to create a beautiful world!

TABLE OF CONTENTS

DEDICATION

This book is dedicated to my Great-Grandma.
Your soft, gentle hands will never be forgotten.

ACKNOWLEDGEMENTS

I want to thank my mom for helping me bring the dream of this book to life. I want to also thank my dad for believing in me. Thanks to my best friend Jazmine who has supported me through the whole process of my business. You have never been a hater and you always encourage me. I love you Jazzy. A big "thank you" to my mentor Ms. Yolanda Owens for always encouraging me and my mentor Ms. Tamara Zantell for always cheering me on. Because of you both, the process of starting and growing my business has been a lot of fun. I would like to thank Ms. Tony, my nail art teacher; your work inspires me and pushes me to get better. Thank you to my sisters, Symona and Sharnae for always taking the best nailfies and for never wearing any other polishes than Sassy G Nail Paints. You guys are the best.

A great big thank you to all of my nail friends, I created this book for you. Let's go create a beautiful world!

INTRODUCTION

Hello! Wait, that's too formal.

Let's try that again.

Hey girl! Welcome to my world.

You are now officially a Sassy G nail friend.

My name is Saniyya Hunt, I am the CEO and chief creator of Sassy G Nailz. I am also the creator of this book. I love beauty and color, I love designing and creating, and I am extremely passionate about kindness.

Kindness is one of those things that can solve a host of problems, but I also know that it takes a lot of confidence to be kind. I believe one of the best ways to build self-confidence is to have well-manicured nails. That is why I started my business and it is also the motivation behind this book.

In this book you will learn everything you need, to maintain beautiful nails. You will discover how to properly take care of your nails and hands as well as learn how to properly paint and design your nails.

All of the pictures and designs in this book are created by my own hands. They aren't perfect, but I am very proud of them. I chose to use my nails and my work rather than a professional because I want to teach girls to be comfortable in their own skin and confident in their ability to create beautiful nails.

It is my mission to create a beautiful world, through kindness, creativity and leadership. As you read this book and learn more about your hands, I hope you also come to understand the power your touch possesses. Through this understanding I hope you will use the power of your hands to be the change you want to see in the world, to connect with people and spread kindness around like glitter nail polish! Together we can be a powerful movement of girls who change the world one manicure at a time.

Remember, Be Kind, Be Confident, and Create a Beautiful world.

5

HOW TO USE THIS BOOK

This book is called the Ultimate Nail Care Guide for Teens because I have spent the last four years searching for one book with everything you need for proper nail care in one place, but I've never found that book. So I decided to create it. I present to you " The Ultimate Nail Care Guide."

In this book you will find everything you need to grow and maintain beautiful nails that look amazing with or without nail polish!

Now, you might think that manicurists or nail technicians are the only people who can create the polished look you desire, but that isn't the whole truth. Yes, they are professionals and have been trained to provide the perfect manicure, but you also have the ability to maintain beautiful hands. There are just a few things you need to know and then practice.

I encourage you to use this book as a guide, use it to find answers to questions you have, use it to inform you on things you don't know, use it to stimulate your creativity, and use it to build confidence in your ability to create amazing nail designs.

New to Nail Care
If you are new to caring for your nails be sure to begin with section 1. These chapters cover the anatomy of your hands and provide a complete guide to nail care essentials. The nail essentials chapter will help you create a supply list. This list has everything you need to maintain your nails. Understanding your hands and how they work is the best way to make decisions about the products you use to maintain their beautiful appearance.

Pretty and Pampered
If you are ready to dive into the world of pampered hands be sure to check out Section 2: The Perfect Manicure. This section provides the steps and sassy tips for creating the perfect manicure. This is one of my favorite sections. It has my favorite hand soak recipe to soften cuticles and a gentle sugar scrub recipe to reveal new glowing skin. It also provides a completely amazing step-by-step guide for polishing flawless, streak-free nails.

The Nail Designer
The last section in this book is all about allowing your imagination and creativity to run free! I have created 10 fun and beautiful nail art designs that you can use to decorate your nails. Every nail design is easy to create and uses only 2 nail tools. The blank nail templates create a space for endless possibilities and endless ideas to take shape. Got an idea? Sketch it out, practice it and then try it on your nails.

SECTION 1:
THE BASICS

"IT TAKES CONFIDENCE TO BE KIND."
- Saniyya Hunt

I remember the day my mom asked me, "Why are bullies so mean?" I had never really thought about it so I said the first thing that came to mind, "Probably because they have low self-esteem." Even though I said it without thinking, I really do think that is the reason. Being mean is the easiest way to protect yourself and hide your insecurities, but being kind is another story.

Being kind takes a lot of courage. You don't know how the person you're showing kindness to will respond and when you are kind to someone who doesn't respond in a nice way, it's kind of embarrassing. When you are kind, especially to strangers or in a new situation, you are showing that you are really brave and really confident in yourself.

So, if you want to be kind you have to be confident and I believe one of the best ways to build self-confidence is by having well-manicured hands. When your hands look good, you feel good and when you feel good, you are more confident.

To have beautiful hands and nails, you first have to understand how your hands are made and how they work. This section will cover the basic anatomy of your hands, the essential tools and products you need to care for your nails and how to determine the best shape for your nails. By understanding the basics, you will be able to make good choices about your hands and you will always know the best way to care for them.

CHAPTER 1

YOUR HANDS

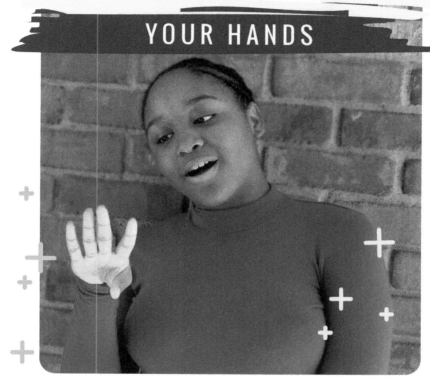

Look at your hands. What do you see?

Your hands are extremely important. You use them more than any other organ on your body. Each of your hands has a palm. Extending from the palm are four fingers and a thumb. The human hand has 27 main bones and at the tip of each digit is a nail.

Hands are also important for their sense of touch. They are very sensitive to different textures and temperatures. When we touch another person, we can share positive energy, this energy can encourage, comfort or even make them feel safe. Your hands have super powers!

SKIN

Your hands and the rest of your body is covered with skin. your skin is your body's largest organ and it is VERY important.

The skin is made up of three layers. The layer on the outside is called the **epidermis** (say: eh-pih-DUR-mis). The epidermis is the part of your skin you can see. Even though you can't see anything happening, your epidermis is doing a lot.

At the bottom of the epidermis, new skin cells are growing. When the new cells are ready, they start moving toward the top of the epidermis. As new cells continue to move up, the older cells near the top die and rise to the surface of the skin. What you see on your hands (and everywhere else on your body) are actually dead skin cells. Eventually, the old skin cells flake and fall off of your body.

THE LAYERS OF YOUR SKIN

- Epidermis
- Dermis
- Subcutaneous Fat

Most of the cells in your epidermis work to make new skin cells. The other cells make a substance called **melanin** (say: MEL-uh-nun). Melanin gives skin its color. The darker your skin, the more melanin you have. Melanin protects your skin from the sun's harmful UltraViolet (UV) rays.

The next layer down is the **dermis** (say: DUR-mis). You can't see your dermis because it's hidden under your epidermis.

The dermis contains nerve endings, blood vessels, and oil and sweat glands. The dermis also contains collagen and elastin to keep the skin looking healthy.

The oil glands in your dermis are called **sebaceous** (say: sih-BAY-shus) **glands**, and they produce **sebum** (say: SEE-bum). Sebum is your skin's natural oil. It rises to the surface of your epidermis to keep your skin lubricated and protected.

The third and bottom layer of the skin is called the **subcutaneous** (say: sub-kyoo-TAY-nee-us) **layer.** It is made mostly of fat and helps your body stay warm and absorb shock.

NAILS

I love my nails. They are my favorite body part! Finger nails are strong, powerful and beautiful. Not only are your nails beautiful they are also very wise. Your fingernails give the doctor an idea about the overall health of your body. They are like a window into your body. By looking at your nails, the doctor can find changes that may be associated with skin problems, lung disease, anemia, and other medical conditions.

Nails start to grow at the nail root hidden under the cuticle. Nails themselves are made of **keratin** (say: KAIR-uh-tin). When cells at the root of the nail grow, the new nail cells push out the old nail cells.

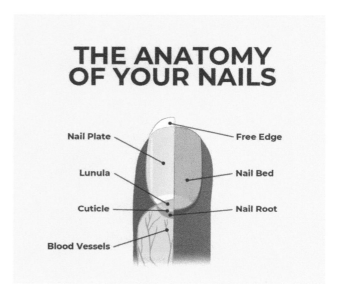

THE ANATOMY OF YOUR NAILS

Nail Plate — Free Edge
Lunula — Nail Bed
Cuticle — Nail Root
Blood Vessels

The place where your nail meets your skin is the cuticle. Some nail techs like to cut the cuticle, but DO NOT let them do it! Cuticles help to protect the new growing nail and the blood vessels feeding the nail root.

The **lunula** (say: LOON-yuh-luh) is that pale half circle just above the cuticle. Your lunula is like a window into your body and is easiest to see on your thumbnail.

Like I said, your hands are beautiful and incredible. Hands do so much for us and are a key part of who we are. In order to maintain fabulously soft hands along with strong, healthy, and sassy nails, we have to take care for them. Keep reading to discover everything you need to care for your hands and nails.

CHAPTER 2

NAIL CARE ESSENTIALS
(The Sassy Girl Nail Kit)

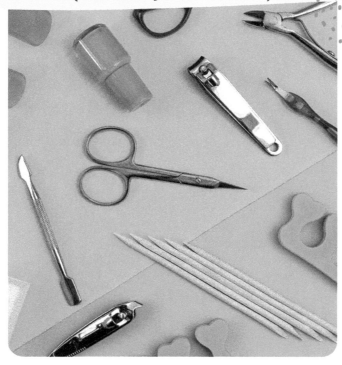

Every girl needs a nail care kit. I call my kit The Sassy Girl Nail Kit. My Sassy Girl Nail Kit has all of the things I use to keep my hands and nails looking amazing. While you don't have to call your kit a Sassy Girl Kit you should definitely give it a name (it's a lot of fun)!

Putting together your nail care kit is the first thing you must do to maintain beautiful and healthy nails. This chapter is your complete nail care supply list and it is broken down into two sections, products and tools. I will list and define all the essentials you'll need for your nail care kit. I have also created an easy to use checklist you can take with you on your next visit to the beauty supply store.

PRODUCTS

CLEANSERS

Cleansers are surfactants that break down dirt and germs so they can be rinsed away with water. Always use a gentle cleanser that doesn't dry out your skin. I use castile soap. Castile soap is made with oil. It is usually made with olive oil, but it can also be made with coconut, castor, or hemp oils. Castile soap is natural and nontoxic which is always a win for me.

NAIL AND HAND SOAK

You need to keep your hands moisturized and your nails strong. Soaks are a great way to do both. Soaks are a mixture of ingredients placed in some kind of carrier liquid like water or oil. Resting yours hands in the proper combination of ingredients can support healthy nail hygiene and growth. There are many soaks you can purchase in the stores, but it's always more fun to create your own.

CUTICLE SOFTENERS AND PROTECTANTS

Our cuticles are important and we do not want to remove them. Instead we should soften and push them back to reveal the full nail bed. Our cuticles are also very delicate and must be protected. This is why cuticle oil is essential for every Sassy Girl.

▷ ▷ ▷ ▷ ▷ SCRUBS

Scrubs are physical exfoliants that rub away dead skin cells. The "feel" of a scrub typically comes from a combination of sugar or salt in an oil base. Hand scrubs are different from body scrubs. Hand scrubs are made with finer sugar crystals than body scrubs which makes them more gentle. Packed with oils, hand scrubs moisturize by removing the dead skin cells that lay on the top layer of skin and allow humectants to absorb into the skin.

MOISTURIZERS

Moisturizers are cosmetic products used for protecting, moisturizing, and lubricating the skin. Moisturizers are important because they help keep your skin from getting dehydrated and damaged. Moisturizers usually incorporate a combination of 3 specific kinds of ingredients: **humectants, emollients, and occlusives.** Humectants draw water to skin cells, emollients are space fillers that fill in the cracks on the skin and occlusive seal in moisture.

NAIL POLISH REMOVER

Nail polish remover is a solvent that breaks down the hard polymer created when nail polish dries. The most common nail polish remover is made with acetone or ethyl acetate. Research has shown that many of the ingredients in nail polish remover causes irritation of the skin, eyes and lungs and also have cancer causing ingredients. I use nail polish solvents that are created using non-toxic oils. These nail polish removers not only break down nail polish they also moisturize the nails.

▷ ▷ ▷ ▷ ▷ NAIL POLISH

Nail Polish is made with a mix of polymers that form a thin, hard film when the acetate evaporates. Most nail polishes include harmful chemicals like DBP, Formaldehyde and Camphor. There are 3-Free, 5-Free, and 10-Free polishes. 3-free polishes are ok because they don't use the 3 most toxic chemicals but 10-free polishes are free from 10 of the most toxic chemicals and animal products used in nail polish. 10-Free polishes are a great product to use to keep your delicate nails looking amazing and your body safe.

BEAUTY AND ESSENTIAL OILS

Beauty oils are thick oils that soften skin and lock in moisture. Essential oils are thinner oils that are extracted from plants. Different oils serve different purposes and should be used to keep your hands healthy and beautiful.

- **Jojoba Oil** is the oil that best mimics your skin's natural sebum and it is amazing!
- **Sesame Oil** kills harmful germs and stops their growth. Sesame oil reduces inflammation and minimizes swelling.
- **Olive Oil** helps in the absorption of calcium. Olive Oil improves the process of calcification and helps nails grow faster.
- **Sweet Almond Oil** helps to make nails healthy by coating them with rich nutrients that protect them from cracking and breaking.
- **Avocado Oil** helps skin stay smooth, strong, and elastic. It also calms itchy skin and protects against skin damage.
- **Myrrh Essential Oil** is one of the best essential oils for nail growth. Myrrh strengthens nails and promotes the growth of smoother, less rigid nails
- **Tea Tree Oil** prevents germs and helps repair damaged nails.
- **Clove Oil** is an anti-fungal oil that helps to heal and prevent infections.

TOOLS

NAIL CLIPPER

A nail clipper is a hand tool used to shorten fingernails. When choosing a nail clipper be sure to choose one that is sturdy and gives a clean cut. Many of the cheaper clippers will flatten the nail and create a cut that doesn't completely separate the nail. I file my nails to shorten and trim them so I don't use a nail clipper often.

NAIL FILE

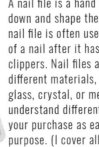

A nail file is a hand tool used to gently grind down and shape the edges of fingernails. A nail file is often used to complete the shape of a nail after it has been trimmed with nail clippers. Nail files are made of many different materials, emery boards, ceramic, glass, crystal, or metal. It is good to understand different file grits before making your purchase as each grit has a specific purpose. (I cover all of that in Chapter 4)

CUTICLE PUSHER ▷▷▷▷▷

A cuticle pusher is a hand tool used to push the cuticle off the nail bed without ripping or damaging the delicate skin on your fingers. Cuticle pushers are made of either wood or metal. I use a wooden cuticle pusher because it feels more gentle against my skin.

NAIL ART BRUSH

A nail art brush is another tool used in creating nail art. The nail art brush has sturdy bristles that can be used to create basic shapes or intricate designs. There are many different shapes and sizes of nail art brushes. For the designs in this book I use a thin brush with fine bristles called a detailing brush.

DOTTING TOOL

The dotting tool is used when creating nail art on your fingernails and is incredibly easy to use. It has a long handle with a small round ball at each tip.

ACRYLIC PAINT

Many nail art designers use acrylic paint to create nail designs. I don't use acrylics much because they don't have a shiny finish but they are nice to have when you want to add small details to your design. All of the designs in this ᵇ are created with nail polish only.

CREATING YOUR NAIL CARE KIT:

Putting it all together

Before you head out to purchase your supplies, evaluate your hands and nails to determine the products and tools you need. Ask yourself these basic questions to help you make decisions about the products you should buy.

What are your nail care goals?
Do you want to maintain natural nails or will you wear artificial nails? Wearing artificial nails can be hard on your nails and the chemicals can be drying. Make sure you have everything you need to keep your nails moisturized.

Do you want to wear your nails long or short? If you want to grow your nails long be sure you have
everything you need to keep your nails strong and also very clean, germs love to hide under longer nails.

Is your skin dry, oily, or a combination of both?
If your skin is dry, consider a moisturizer that is both an emollient and an occlusive. If you have oily skin consider a moisturizer that is more of a humectant, and if you have combination skin consider a moisturizer that is a balance of all three.

What oils are best for your hands and nails?
Remember, Jojoba oil mimics the oil your body produces naturally. Sesame oil reduces inflammation and acts like a barrier. Olive Oil is a healing oil and prevents nail breakage. Sweet Almond oil helps to restore nail health and Avocado Oil promotes collagen production and helps grow new skin.

What essential oils will help you achieve your nail care goals?
Lavender oil helps to strengthen nails and cuticles. Myrrh protects nails from becoming brittle and thin. Tea Tree oil prevents germs and helps repair damaged nails. Clove oil is an anti-fungal oil that helps to heal and prevent infections.

How will you keep everything organized?
I have a really cute carrying case where I keep all of my supplies. I found my case at Target but you can find yours anywhere. The one tip I will share is to make sure you find a case that stands up, can be wiped off and is waterproof.

15

NAIL CARE ESSENTIALS

HAND PRODUCTS

- ☐ GENTLE HAND CLEANSER
- ☐ HAND SCRUB
- ☐ MOISTURIZER
- ☐ CUTICLE OIL

NAIL PRODUCTS

- ☐ NAIL POLISH
- ☐ NAIL POLISH REMOVER
- ☐ OILS
- ☐ ESSENTIAL OILS

TOOLS

- ☐ NAIL CLIPPER
- ☐ NAIL FILE
- ☐ CUTICLE PUSHER
- ☐ DOTTING TOOL
- ☐ NAIL ART BRUSH
- ☐ ACRYLIC PAINT (OPTIONAL)

(You may print your FREE PDF on my website www.sassygnailz.com **CODE: SassyGirl**)

CHAPTER 3

THE PERFECT SHAPE

While I love beautiful nail polish colors, the foundation of gorgeous nails is the shape. Some girls love to follow the latest trend, but wearing the wrong shape nails can make your manicure look less than perfect. The correct shape can flatter your whole hand and make it appear more attractive. The shape of your nails has more power than you might think. This is why choosing the best nail shape for your fingers is an important task you shouldn't skip.

5 CLASSIC NAIL SHAPES

SQUARE   ROUND   OVAL   ALMOND   BALLERINA

When choosing a nail shape, you should know the different options available. Although there are many variations, there are five basic shapes; square, round, oval, almond, and ballerina. To figure out which style is best for you, you should think about your palm width, finger length, nail bed length, and desired nail length.

SQUARE

Square-shaped nails are also perfect for shorter nails. Square nails are created by filing straight edges and a squared tip. Square shaped nails are flattering for those with thin hands and long, slim fingers. This shape also breaks less which makes it perfect for active girls.

ROUND

If you want to create the appearance of longer fingers but like to keep your nails short, you should consider a round shape. Round shaped nails, which have a short length with a naturally curved edge, are perfect for subtly making short and wide fingers look longer. The shape can also be used to make wide nail beds appear thinner and longer.

OVAL

Thanks to their elongating abilities, oval shaped nails are perfect for both short and wide nail beds and fingers. The medium to long shape, which ends in a semi-circle, is similar to almond styles except blunter and more delicate in appearance. The result is a sassy nail shape that helps to make wide fingers appear slimmer and short fingers look longer.

ALMOND

Almond-shaped nails feature slim sides, which taper towards the end, and have a rounded tip. This shape looks really nice on longer nail lengths and is also great for making wide fingers look slender to create the appearance of slim hands and long nails beds.

BALLERINA

One of the best shapes for long nail lovers and those with narrow nail beds is the ballerina shape. Begin by filing the side walls to a point. Then, file the tip straight just as you would a square nail.While this shape is beautiful, girls should only attempt to wear this shape if their nails are long and sturdy. Short and brittle nails may not be able to handle this shape.

WHAT NAIL SHAPE IS PERFECT FOR YOU?

Take a look at your hands and consider three things; the length of your fingers, the length of your nail beds and the width of your palm. Use this fun little chart to narrow in on your perfect nail shape.

FIND YOUR PERFECT SHAPE

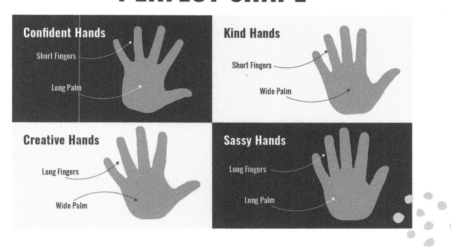

Confident Hands
(Long Palm, Short Fingers)
Best nail shape: Oval. This shape will help make your fingers appear longer and thinner to balance out the length of your palm. File the sides of your nails straight and gently taper the free edge into a semicircle.

Kind Hands
(Wide Palm, Short Fingers)
Best nail shape: Almond and Oval. Tapered shapes like the almond shaped nail, elongate shorter or wider fingers. I recommend you opt for rounded shapes in general, especially if you have a wide nail bed.

Creative Hands
(Wide Palm, Long Fingers)
Best nail shape: Ballerina. The edgy ballerina shape is enhanced by long fingers and balanced by a square palm. They do require sturdy nails and regular TLC to avoid breakages.

Sassy Hands
(Long Palm, Long Fingers)
Best nail shape: Square. You can get away with wearing this blunt look at any length. And they are one of the more practical, low-maintenance shapes to wear to school.

SECTION 2:

SELF-CARE IS THE BEST CARE

"LIFE ISN'T PERFECT, BUT YOUR NAILS CERTAINLY CAN BE!"

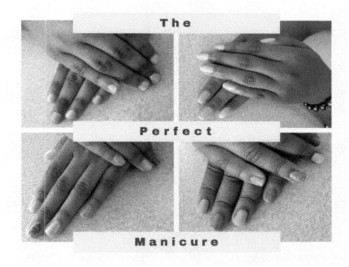

The Perfect Manicure

My mom talks a lot about self-care. She says that self-care is the best care because self-care is about creating a healthy relationship with yourself. Self-care means doing things to take care of your mind, body, and soul through activities that make you feel good, make you happy and reduce stress. When you do self-care activities you allow yourself to live fully, vibrantly, and confidently.

The practice of self-care also helps to remind you that you are beautiful, worthy and a priority. Regularly giving yourself a manicure is a great self-care activity. This section will tell you everything you need to know about giving the best and most relaxing manicure.

CHAPTER 4

THE PERFECT MANICURE

Step 1: Shape your nails

Shaping your nails is the foundation of a great manicure, but using the wrong nail file can destroy your nails. So, before you begin filing and shaping your nails, be sure you are using the correct nail file. Nail files have many different purposes. A nail file is used to shorten the nails, a file is used to shape the nail. A file is also used to smooth and buff the nails. The grit on the file is what determines its purpose. A nail file's grit level is the level of abrasiveness of the surface on the file. The grit level is represented by a number. This number tells you how course or abrasive the surface is. The lower the number the coarser the grit. The numbers range from 50 being the coarsest to 1000 being the smoothest.

This guide will help you choose the perfect nail file!

Special thanks to my Instagram nail friends for helping me with this guide. Be sure to follow them, they are amazing. @viperlovr, @p10nails, @creatively_danielle, and @ghostlynails

NAIL FILE
GRIT GUIDE

80-150
SHAPING ACRYLIC NAILS

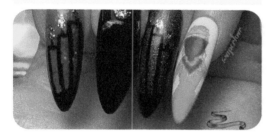

150-180
SHAPING GEL NAILS

180-240
SHAPING NATURAL NAILS

240-320
SMOOTHING AND BUFFING NAILS

400 AND UP
HIGH SHINE BUFFING

Shape your nails like a professional!

FIRST: Select your perfect nail shape (If you need help with this, be sure to read Chapter 3). Don't be afraid to embrace your natural shape.

SECOND: Think of your nails in two sections, one on the left and one on the right. File your nails in one direction up toward the center on one side and up toward the center on the other side. Do not saw your nails using a back-and-forth motion.

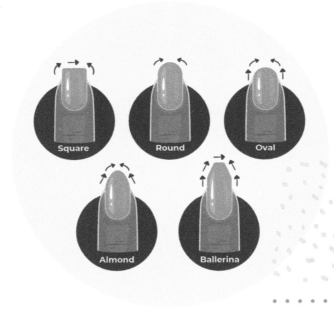

THIRD: Hold the file flat against the nail while filing. If you angle the file, it will make the nail thin and will break easily. File slowly and don't rush.

FINALLY: Smooth and buff the nails so they look flawless.

Sassy Tip: File your nails over a dark surface so you can see them better.

Step 2: Soak it all in!

SASSY AND SOFT HAND SOAK

Ingredients

3 cups of warm water
½ cup of baking soda
½ cup of Epsom salt
4-6 drops of lavender essential oil

Directions

1. Mix dry ingredients in a large bowl.
2. Fill a small bowl with warm water.
3. Add 2 scoops of powder mix to warm water and soak hands for 10-15 mins.

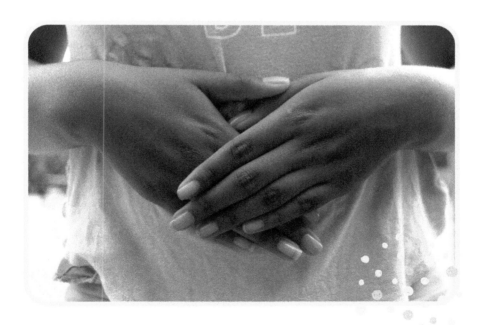

SOAK HANDS AND SOFTEN CUTICLES

Our cuticles grow along our nail plate and protect our nail root from infections. When we are looking to create a beautiful manicure however, the cuticles can get in the way and cause our nail polish to chip. Softening the cuticles and pushing them back allows the full nail bed to be revealed, creating a beautiful canvas to polish. There are many different nail soaks you can use and each can be used for a different purpose. The Sassy and Soft Hand soak is used to soften the cuticles as well as moisturize the skin on our hands.

FIRST:
Mix the ingredients with warm water and prepare the hand soak.

SECOND:
Allow your hands to rest in the warm water for 10-15 mins.

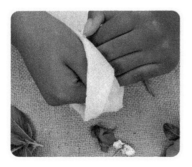

THIRD:
Pat hands lightly dry with a soft towel.

FINALLY:
Use a cuticle pusher to gently push the softened cuticles away from the nail bed.

Step 3: Scrub it all away

SMOOTH AND CONFIDENT SUGAR SCRUB

Ingredients

1 Cup Sugar
¼ cup Jojoba Oil
¼ cup Almond Oil
1tsp Vitamin E Oil
1tsp castile soap
4-6 drops tea tree essential oil

Directions

1. Place sugar into a small jar
2. Add castile soap
3. Add carrier oils to the jar
4. Add essential oils and
   mix ingredients together

SCRUB AND SMOOTH CUTICLES AND DEAD SKIN CELLS

Part of the perfect manicure is having naturally soft skin. Hands that are smooth and radiant are also confident hands. A simple way to achieve this confident, smooth and radiant look is through exfoliation. Exfoliation is when you remove the outer layer of dead skin cells. A gentle sugar scrub is a perfect way to exfoliate skin. When creating your own sugar scrub, be sure to use finely granulated sugar to ensure it is not too abrasive.

FIRST:

Dampen skin and rub sugar scrub over the hands as well as the cuticles on the nail beds.

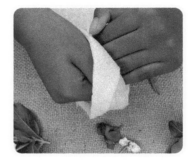

NEXT:

Rinse hands completely and pat dry.

FINALLY:

Finish with a nutrient rich hand oil.

Step 4: Polish the Nails

I love self-care. I love experiencing and giving myself manicures. I love the shaping, the soaking and scrubbing, but more than all of that, my FAVORITE part of the manicure is polishing my nails.

I love nail polish. So many colors and so many options. Most nail polishes include harmful chemicals like DBP, Formaldehyde and Camphor but 10-free polishes are free from 10 of the most toxic chemicals and animal products used in nail polish. This makes 10-Free polishes a great product to use to keep our delicate nails looking amazing and your body safe. Sassy G Nailz is a 10-Free, vegan polish line with tons of fast drying and vibrant colors.

STEP 4: POLISH THE NAILS

There is an art to polishing your nails! The perfect manicure must look smooth and streak-free. Let me show you how to achieve that look!

FIRST:
Choose your nail polish

NEXT:
Apply a base coat of clear nail polish

THIRD:
Place a drop of paint at the bottom of the nails. Next, dip the brush in the drop of polish at the base of the nail and pull the brush upwards in a straight line through the center of the nail all the way to the tip. Repeat this on the left side of the nail and again on the right.

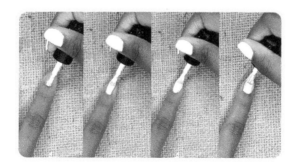

FINALLY:
Use the brush to paint the tip of the nail.

Sassy Tip: When polishing your dominant hand, roll your fingers on a sturdy surface instead of trying to move the brush around the nail bed. This will help you create smoother and cleaner strokes.

SECTION 3:

NAIL ART

**"CHASE YOUR DREAMS FEARLESSLY WITH
A BEAUTIFUL SET OF NAILS!"**

It's time to take your manicure to the next level! Let's transform your traditional manicure to one that is sassy, bold and creative!!!

This section is all about nail art. All of the designs have been created by my hands. The designs are created and demonstrated using clear artificial nails. I like practicing on fake nails because it allows me to perfect a technique before attempting a design on my freshly painted nails. Use these easy-to-follow nail art tutorials as inspiration for your next manicure masterpiece.

+ + +

CHAPTER 5

DIY DESIGNS

ONE STARRY NIGHT

"EVERY GREAT DREAM BEGINS WITH A DREAMER.
ALWAYS REMEMBER, YOU HAVE WITHIN YOU THE
STRENGTH, THE PATIENCE, AND THE PASSION TO
REACH FOR THE STARS TO CHANGE THE WORLD."

HARRIET TUBMAN

ONE STARRY NIGHT

This design uses an ombre of blue and white as the night time background. Anytime you create ombre nail art, a thin layer of peel off liquid latex is a great way to keep the skin around the nails clean.

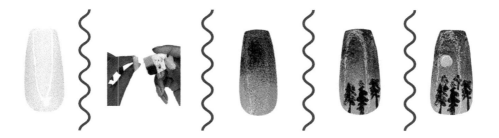

Step 1: Begin with a white nail polish foundation.

Step 2: Add blue and white nail polish to a make-up sponge. Gently stamp the sponge on the nail. Ensure the white polish end of the sponge is at the cuticle edge of the nails. (Be careful not to press down too hard with the sponge).

Step 3: Using a thin detailing brush, paint black trees at the base of the nails.

Step 4: Using a dotting tool, add a white moon to the free edge of the nail.

Step 5: Lightly sponge on silver glitter polish to create a starry sparkle.

Step 6: Seal the design with a clear top coat once your art is completely dry.

COOKIES AND CREAM

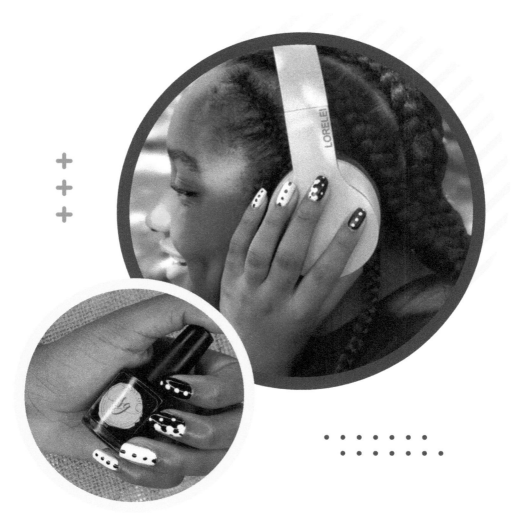

"SNACKS ALWAYS TASTE BETTER WHEN YOUR
MANICURE IS FLAWLESS."

TERRI HUNT

COOKIES AND CREAM

Step 1: Begin with a white nail polish foundation.

Step 2: Polish a black overlay across the white base. (Don't worry about making it straight, be creative!)

Step 3: Using a dotting tool, place black dots where the black and white polishes meet. Be sure to space out dots, leaving room in between the black dots.

Step 4: Using a dotting tool, add white polish between the black dots.

Step 5: Using the dotting tool, detail the white side with black dots and the black side with white dots.

Step 6: Seal the design with a clear top coat once your art is completely dry.

BEAR CLAWS

"IT IS IN YOUR HANDS TO CREATE A BETTER
WORLD FOR ALL WHO LIVE IN IT."

NELSON MANDELA

BEAR CLAWS

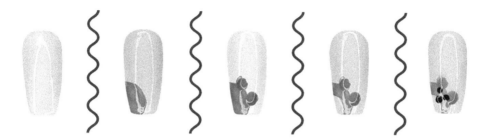

Step 1: Begin with a white nail polish foundation.

Step 2: Select a color for your bear and use your detailing brush to draw a half circle at the corner of the nail's free edge.

Step 3: Using the dotting tool, place two dots of the same color at the top of the half circle

Step 4: Use the detailing brush to draw a smaller half circle using white polish inside the larger half circle.

Step 5: Using the dotting tool, place three black dots inside the circles to create the bear's face.

Step 6: Seal the design with a clear top coat once your art is completely dry.

CELEBRATE

"THE MORE YOU PRAISE AND CELEBRATE YOUR LIFE, THE MORE THERE IS IN LIFE TO CELEBRATE."

OPRAH WINFREY

CELEBRATE

Step 1: Begin with a red nail polish foundation.

Step 2: Using the nail polish brush paint 3 broad strokes at the free edge of the nail (make sure to leave space between each stroke)

Step 3: Using the dotting tool, place three yellow dots above each of the white strokes.

Step 4: Use the detailing brush to drag the polish up from the dot to create a flame.

Step 5: Add details to the candles using your detailing brush.

Step 6: Seal the design with a clear top coat once your art is completely dry.

PAINT PARTY

"THE MOST ALLURING THING A WOMAN
CAN HAVE IS CONFIDENCE."

BEYONCE

PAINT PARTY

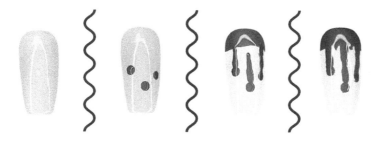

Step 1: Begin with a white nail polish foundation.
Step 2: Select a color for your paint drips.
Step 3: Using the dotting tool, place three dots at different places near the free edge of the nail.
Step 4: Using the dotting tool, drag polish toward the cuticle edge of your nail.
Step 5: Using your nail polish brush, paint the base of your nail and connect the polish with the three long lines.
Step 6: Seal the design with a clear top coat once your art is completely dry.

IN THE WILD

"I GOT MY START BY GIVING MYSELF A START."

MADAM C.J. WALKER

IN THE WILD

This design uses an ombre of yellow, orange and red as the background. Anytime you create ombre nail art, a thin layer of peel off liquid latex is a great way to keep the skin around the nails clean.

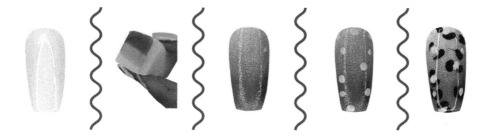

Step 1: Begin with a white nail polish foundation.

Step 2: Add yellow, orange, and red nail polish to a make-up sponge. Gently stamp the sponge on the nail. Ensure the yellow polish end of the sponge is at the cuticle edge of the nails. (Be careful not to press down too hard with the sponge).

Step 3: Using a dotting tool, place white dots randomly on the nail plate.

Step 4: Using your detailing brush, paint a "c" shape on either side of the white dots using black polish.

Step 5: Seal the design with a clear top coat once your art is completely dry.

SPREAD LOVE

"THE MINUTE YOU LEARN TO LOVE YOURSELF,
YOU WON'T WANT TO BE ANYBODY ELSE."

RIHANNA

SPREAD LOVE

Step 1: Begin with a black nail polish foundation.

Step 2: Use your dotting tool to add three white dots in a triangular formation.

Step 3: Using a detailing brush carefully connect the dots, forming the outline of a heart.

Step 4: Using your detailing brush fill in the heart outline with white polish

Step 5: Seal the design with a clear top coat once your art is completely dry.

TRANSFORM AND GLOW

+ + +

. . . .
. . . .

"YOU MUST BE THE CHANGE YOU WANT
TO SEE IN THE WORLD."

MAHATMA GANDHI

TRANSFORM AND GLOW

Step 1: Begin with a blue nail polish foundation.

Step 2: Using a thin detailing brush create an "m" shaped outline using near the tip end of the nail.

Step 3: Using the black nail polish brush, paint the free edge of the nail to fill in space around the outline you've created.

Step 4: Using a dotting tool, add a white dot to the free edge of the nail.

Step 5: Seal the design with a clear top coat once your art is completely dry.

BLOSSOM AND BLOOM

"NEVER BE LIMITED BY OTHER PEOPLE'S
LIMITED IMAGINATIONS."

DR. MAE JEMISON

BLOSSOM AND BLOOM

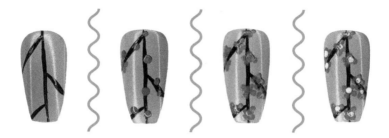

Step 1: Begin with a teal nail polish foundation.

Step 2: Using your detailing brush, paint one black line down the center of the nail. Add three additional black lines coming from the center line.

Step 3: Use the dotting tool to randomly add pink dots to the black lines.

Step 4: Continue to use your dotting tool to add light pink dots around the dark pink dots.

Step 5: Add white dots to the center of each flower using the dotting tool.

Step 6: Seal the design with a clear top coat once your art is completely dry.

PEACE AND GOOD VIBES

+ + +

"YOU WILL BE EXACTLY AS HAPPY
AS YOU DECIDE TO BE!"

COACH P

PEACE AND GOOD VIBES

Step 1: Begin with a white nail polish foundation.

Step 2: Add large drops of red, orange, yellow and blue to the nail. (Try to work fast so the polish doesn't dry)

Step 3: Using a thin detailing brush gently and carefully drag colors so they mix together nicely

Step 4: Seal the design with a clear top coat once your art is completely dry.

CHAPTER 6

DREAM IT AND CREATE IT!

Beautiful nail art is all about creativity, imagination and practice. In this chapter you will find 10 pages of nail templates to fill with design ideas and sketches. Use these pages to practice and have fun. Don't hold back! The best designs happen when you set your mind free to wonder and try new things.

Find additional practice templates on my website www.sassygnailz.com

DESIGN AND CREATE
BEAUTIFUL, SASSY NAIL ART!
Confidence comes through practice!

Almond Nails Practice Page

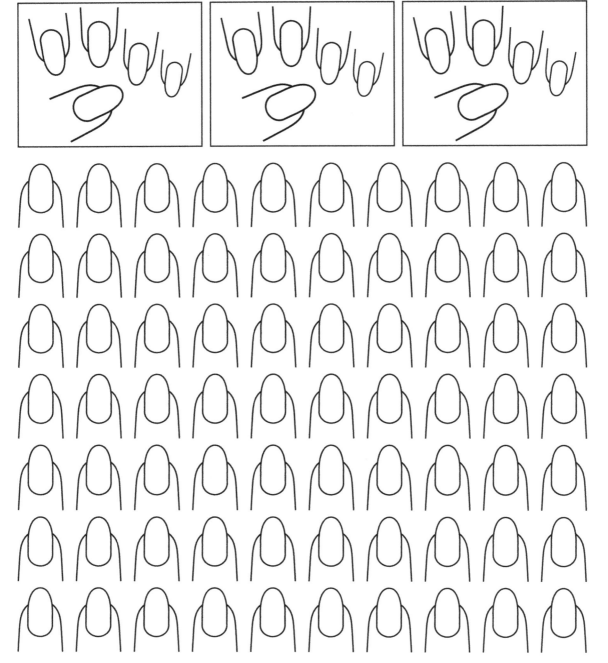

DESIGN AND CREATE
BEAUTIFUL, SASSY NAIL ART!
Confidence comes through practice!

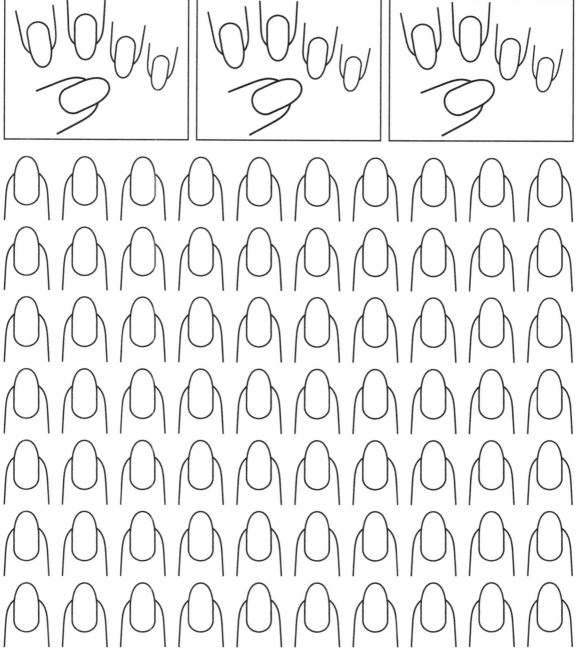

DESIGN AND CREATE
BEAUTIFUL, SASSY NAIL ART!
Confidence comes through practice!

Almond Nails Practice Page

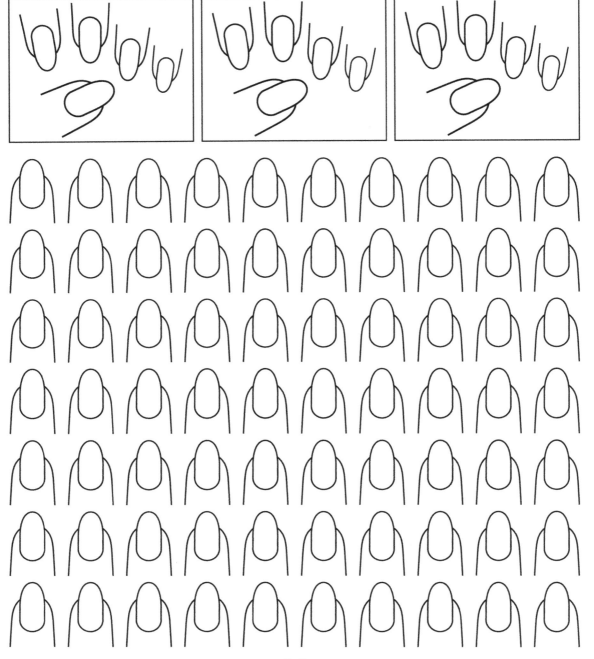

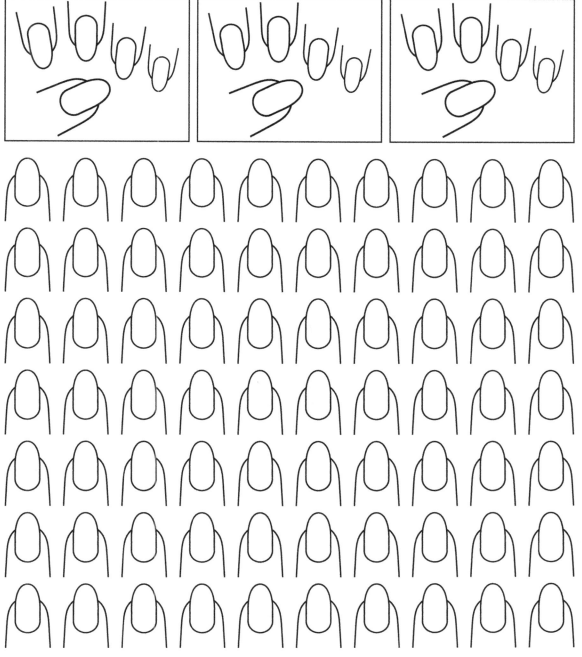

DESIGN AND CREATE
BEAUTIFUL, SASSY NAIL ART!
Confidence comes through practice!

Almond Nails Practice Page

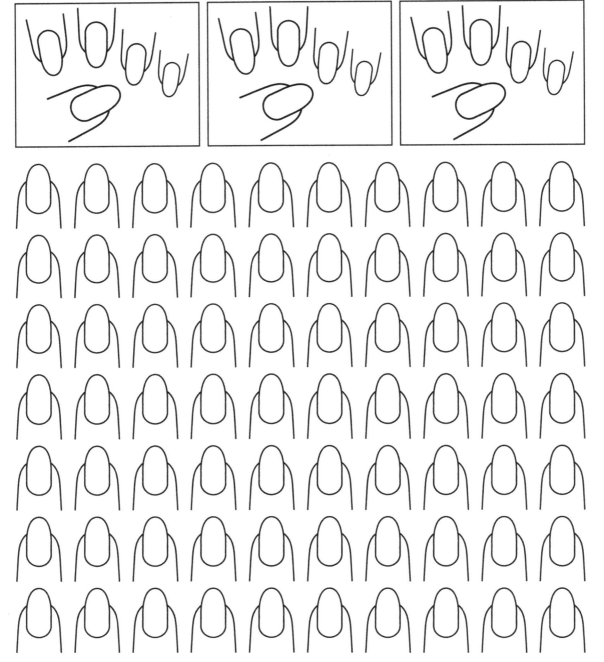

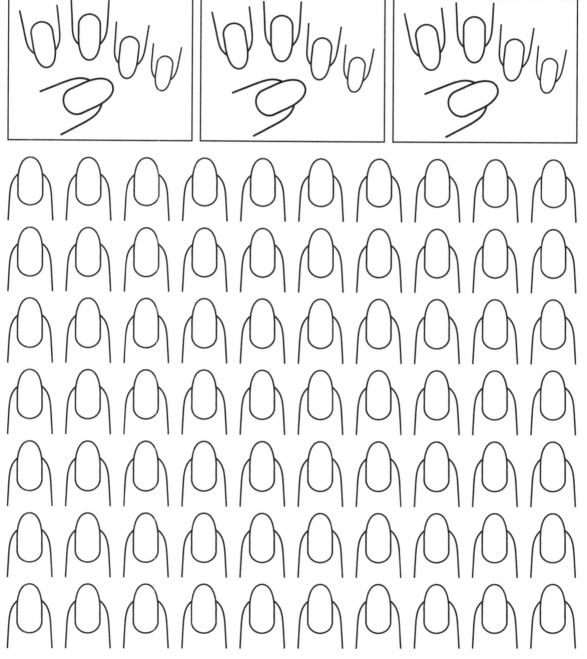

DESIGN AND CREATE
BEAUTIFUL, SASSY NAIL ART!
Confidence comes through practice!

Ballerina Nails Practice Page

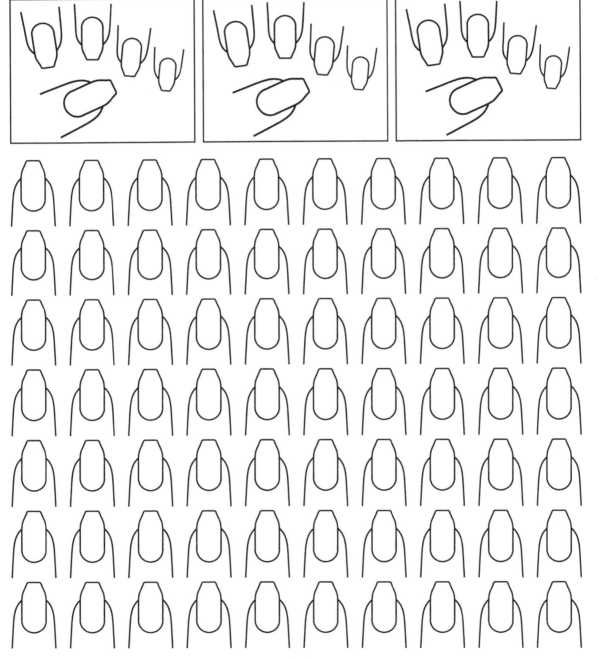

64

DESIGN AND CREATE
BEAUTIFUL, SASSY NAIL ART!
Confidence comes through practice!

Ballerina Nails Practice Page

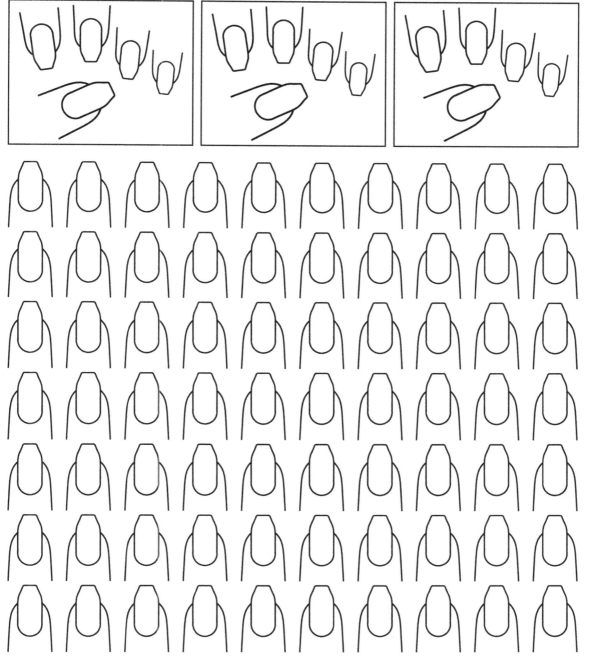

DESIGN AND CREATE
BEAUTIFUL, SASSY NAIL ART!
Confidence comes through practice!

Ballerina Nails Practice Page

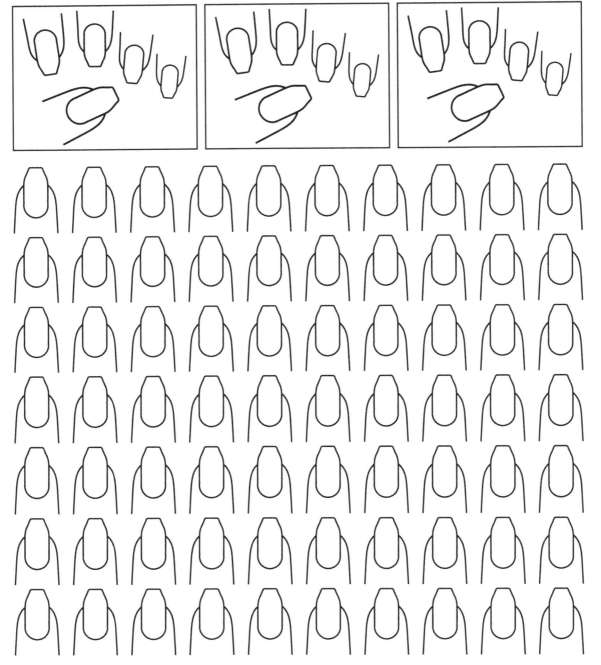

DESIGN AND CREATE
BEAUTIFUL, SASSY NAIL ART!
Confidence comes through practice!

Ballerina Nails Practice Page

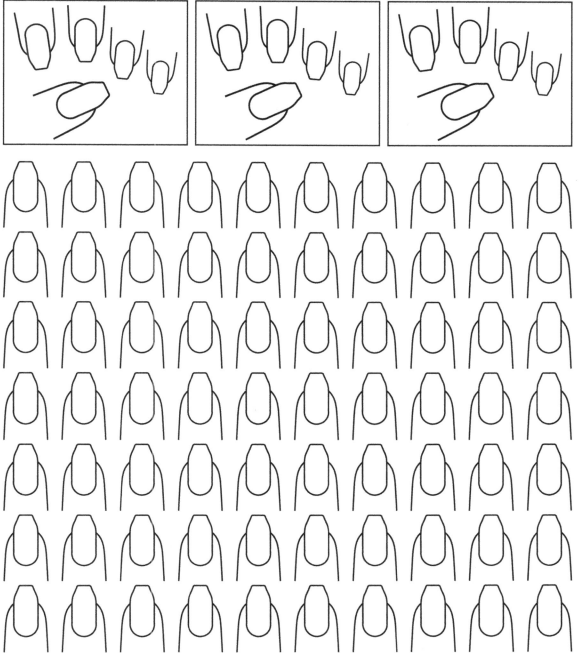

DESIGN AND CREATE
BEAUTIFUL, SASSY NAIL ART!
Confidence comes through practice!

Ballerina Nails Practice Page

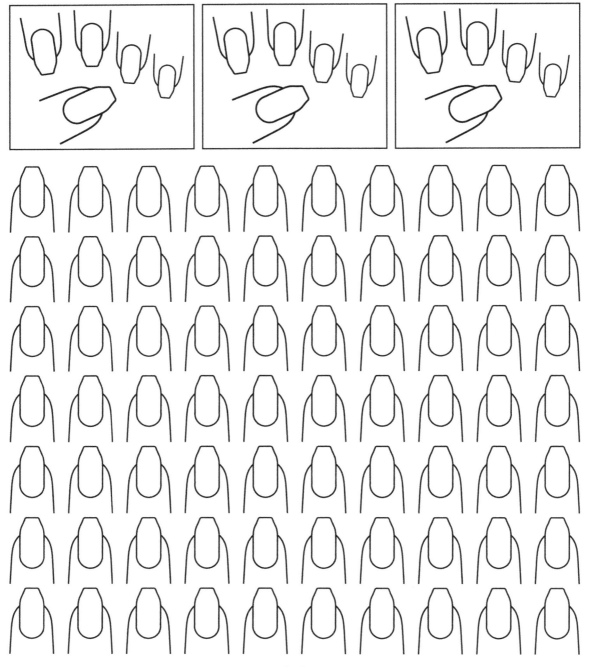

DESIGN AND CREATE
BEAUTIFUL, SASSY NAIL ART!
Confidence comes through practice!

Ballerina Nails Practice Page

DESIGN AND CREATE
BEAUTIFUL, SASSY NAIL ART!
Confidence comes through practice!

Oval Nails Practice Page

DESIGN AND CREATE
BEAUTIFUL, SASSY NAIL ART!
Confidence comes through practice!

Oval Nails Practice Page

DESIGN AND CREATE
BEAUTIFUL, SASSY NAIL ART!
Confidence comes through practice!

72

DESIGN AND CREATE
BEAUTIFUL, SASSY NAIL ART!
Confidence comes through practice!

DESIGN AND CREATE
BEAUTIFUL, SASSY NAIL ART!
Confidence comes through practice!

Oval Nails Practice Page

DESIGN AND CREATE
BEAUTIFUL, SASSY NAIL ART!
Confidence comes through practice!

Oval Nails Practice Page

DESIGN AND CREATE
BEAUTIFUL, SASSY NAIL ART!
Confidence comes through practice!

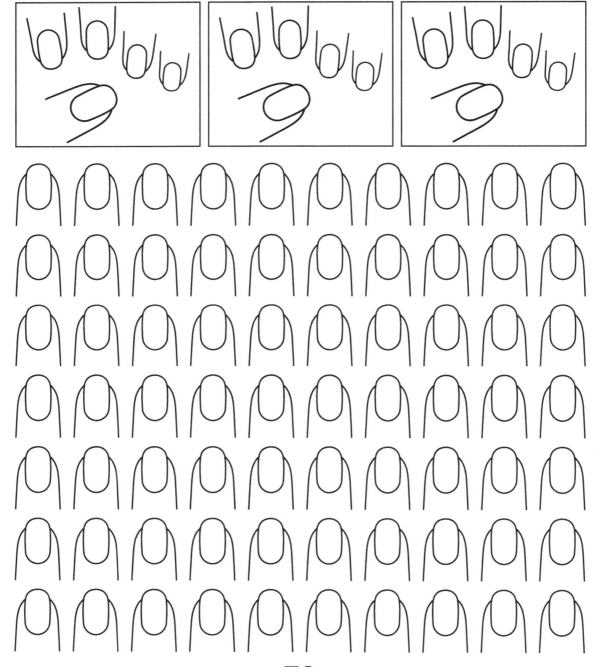

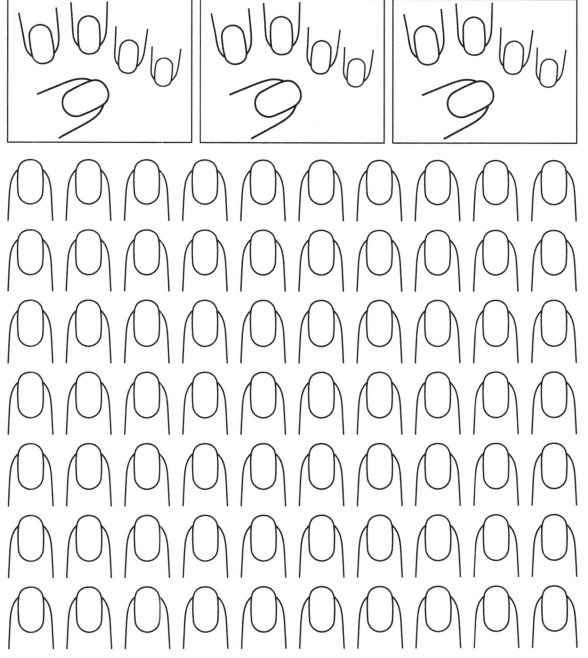

DESIGN AND CREATE
BEAUTIFUL, SASSY NAIL ART!
Confidence comes through practice!

Round Nails Practice Page

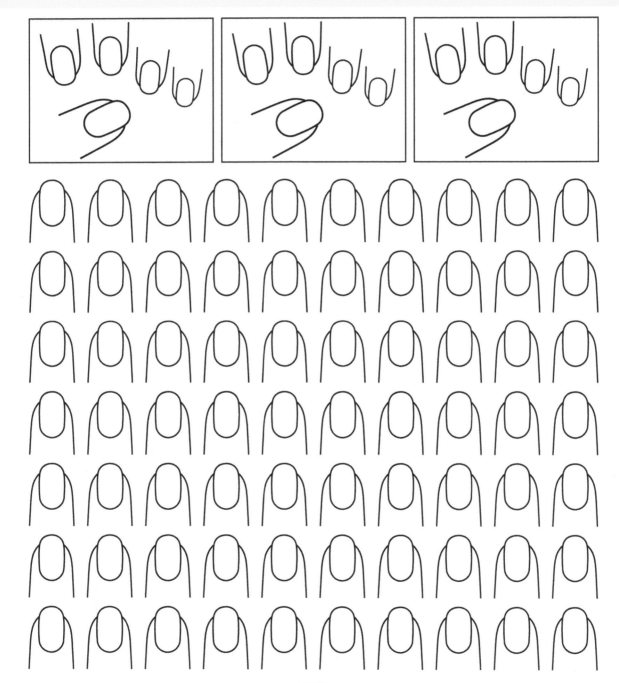

78

DESIGN AND CREATE
BEAUTIFUL, SASSY NAIL ART!
Confidence comes through practice!

Round Nails Practice Page

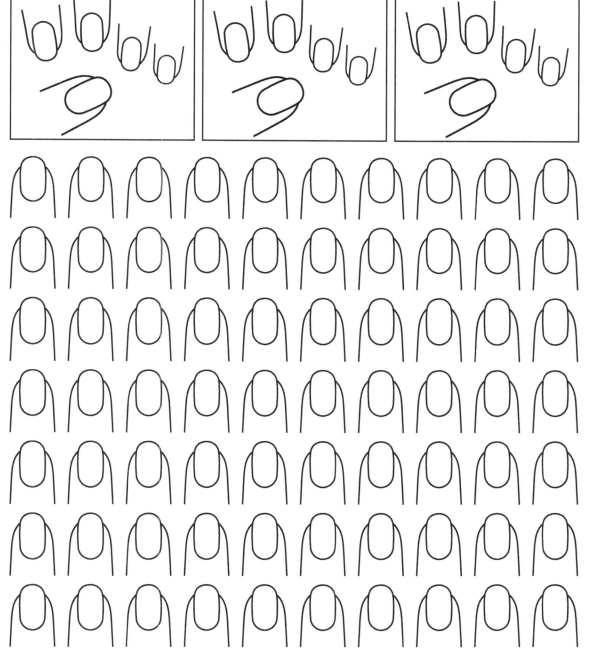

DESIGN AND CREATE
BEAUTIFUL, SASSY NAIL ART!
Confidence comes through practice!

Round Nails Practice Page

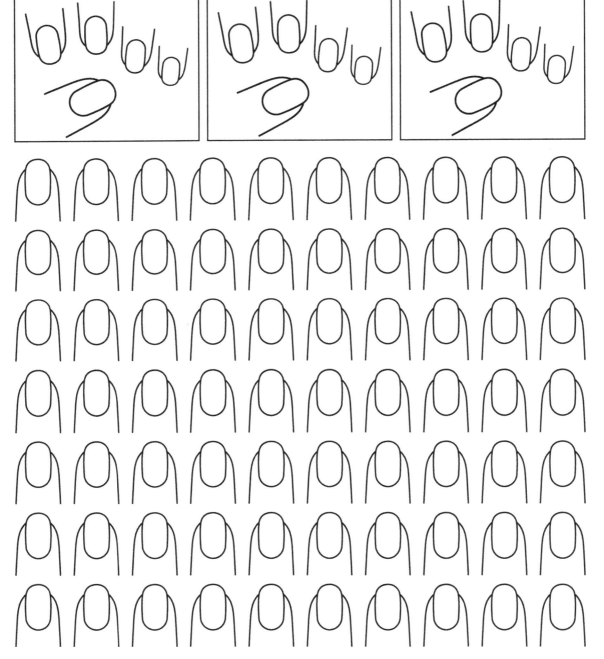

DESIGN AND CREATE
BEAUTIFUL, SASSY NAIL ART!
Confidence comes through practice!

Round Nails Practice Page

DESIGN AND CREATE
BEAUTIFUL, SASSY NAIL ART!
Confidence comes through practice!

Square Nails Practice Page

DESIGN AND CREATE
BEAUTIFUL, SASSY NAIL ART!
Confidence comes through practice!

Square Nails Practice Page

DESIGN AND CREATE
BEAUTIFUL, SASSY NAIL ART!
Confidence comes through practice!

Square Nails Practice Page

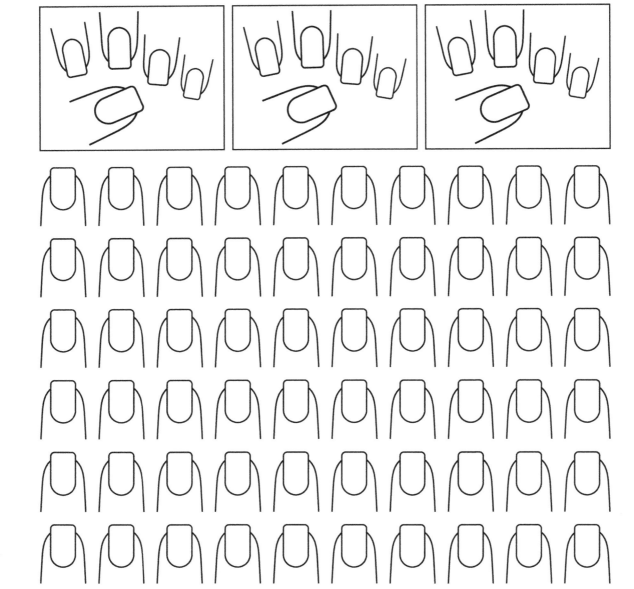

DESIGN AND CREATE
BEAUTIFUL, SASSY NAIL ART!
Confidence comes through practice!

Square Nails Practice Page

DESIGN AND CREATE
BEAUTIFUL, SASSY NAIL ART!
Confidence comes through practice!

Square Nails Practice Page

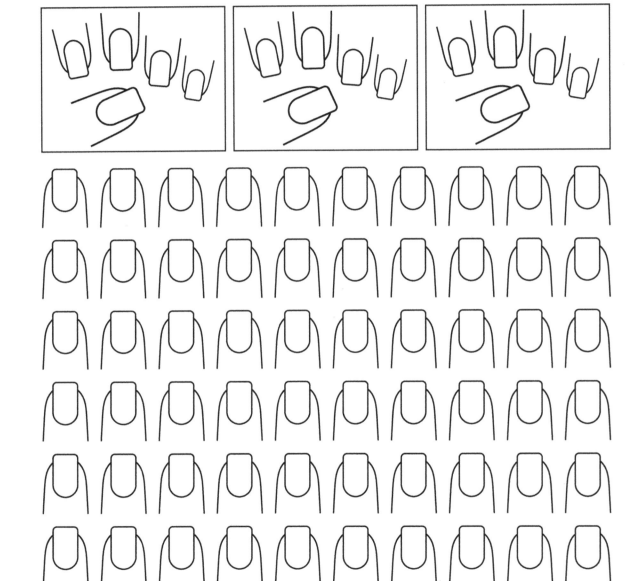

PAY IT FORWARD

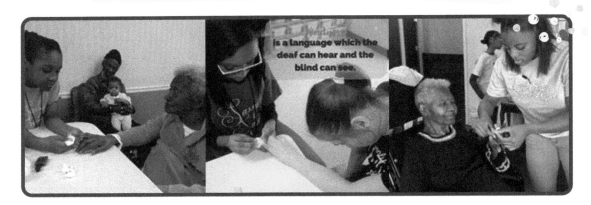

You now know and have everything you need to maintain strong, healthy and fabulously sassy nails.

This is your new super power.

The real question is "what will you do with this super power now that you have it?" With well-manicured nails you will walk with a confidence others will admire. With the knowledge of how to give the perfect manicure you have a gift many will envy. In your hands you have the power to connect and heal, in your hands you have the power of touch.

When I was a little girl, I loved the feel of my Grandma Tillie's hands. After she died, I missed her touch more than anything. I remember visiting a nursing home for the first time. I remember how happy I was to touch the residents' soft hands and how much they loved my touch.

I started The Sassy Squad Project in 2018. The Sassy Squad is a group of my closest friends. Together we visit nursing homes and assisted living facilities to provide free manicures to the residents. Through our service we spread love, we connect through touch and we brighten lives.

With the power you now have in your hands, I am asking you to pay it forward. Give a manicure...
to your mother,
to your grandmother,
to a neighbor
or to someone at your local community center. (if it is safe to do so)

If each of us agree to touch one person, we can spread kindness like glitter and change the world; ONE MANICURE AT A TIME!

Remember, be kind, be confident, and create a beautiful world!

Love ya,
Sassy G (aka Saniyya Hunt)

SKETCH

SKETCH

SKETCH

SKETCH

SKETCH

SKETCH

SKETCH

SKETCH

SKETCH

SKETCH

NOTES

NOTES

NOTES

NOTES

NOTES

NOTES

NOTES

NOTES

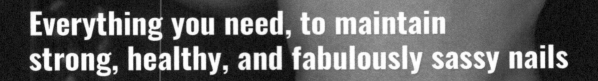

SASSY NAILS

The Ultimate

Nail Care Guide

for Teens

D1736834

Everything you need, to maintain
strong, healthy, and fabulously sassy nails

SANIYYA G. HUNT

NOTES

NOTES

CPSIA information can be obtained
at www.ICGtesting.com
Printed in the USA
LVHW081308110523
746637LV00007B/139

9 781736 694305